coffee

a fine selection of sweet treats

MURDOCH BOOKS

Contents

Morning coffee

Rise and shine to these sweet treats,
guaranteed to kick-start your day.

Little plum cakes with coffee caramel

MAKES 10

150 g (5½ oz) unsalted butter, softened
140 g (5 oz/¾ cup) soft brown sugar
2 eggs
165 g (5¾ oz/1⅓ cups) plain (all-purpose) flour
1½ teaspoons baking powder
¼ teaspoon freshly grated nutmeg
125 g (4½ oz/½ cup) plain yoghurt
3 firm ripe plums or small peaches, halved and thinly sliced

Coffee caramel
170 g (6 oz/¾ cup) caster (superfine) sugar
80 ml (2½ fl oz/⅓ cup) freshly made hot espresso coffee

To make the coffee caramel, place the sugar and 80 ml (2½ fl oz/⅓ cup) water in a small heavy-based saucepan over medium heat and stir to dissolve the sugar. Bring to the boil, without stirring, and cook the syrup until golden brown. Immediately remove from the heat, carefully pour in the coffee—beware, the caramel will splutter and spit—and stir to combine. Transfer to a heatproof jug and set aside.

Preheat the oven to 180°C (350°F/Gas 4). Grease ten 125 ml (4 fl oz/½ cup) friand tins.

Cream the butter and sugar in a large bowl using electric beaters until pale and fluffy. Add the eggs, one at a time, beating well after each addition. Sift in the flour, baking powder and nutmeg, then add the yoghurt and mix well. Spoon the batter into the prepared tins and arrange the fruit slices on top. Bake for 20–25 minutes, or until a skewer inserted in the centre of a cake comes out clean. Turn out onto a wire rack to cool.

Serve the cakes warm with a drizzle of coffee caramel.

Almond espresso biscotti

Preheat the oven to 180°C (350°F/Gas 4). Line two baking trays with baking paper.

Sift the flour, baking powder, salt and ground coffee into a large bowl, then stir in the almonds. Combine the eggs, orange zest, almond essence and sugar in a separate bowl and mix well. Make a well in the centre of the dry ingredients. Gradually pour in the egg mixture and stir with a wooden spoon until the mixture just comes together to form a dough.

Divide the dough into quarters and, using lightly floured hands, shape each portion into a 3 x 25 cm (1¼ x 10 inch) log. Transfer the logs to the prepared trays. Bake for 15–20 minutes, or until slightly risen and lightly golden. Set aside to cool for 10 minutes. Cut the logs into 5 mm (¼ inch) thick slices using a serrated knife. Place the biscotti well apart in a single layer on the trays. Return to the oven and bake for 15 minutes, turning the biscotti halfway through cooking time. Allow to cool on the trays for a few minutes, then transfer to a wire rack to cool completely.

MAKES 60

250 g (9 oz/2 cups) plain (all-purpose) flour
½ teaspoon baking powder
pinch of salt
1 tablespoon finely ground espresso
   coffee beans
115 g (4 oz/¾ cup) whole almonds, toasted
   and chopped
3 eggs, lightly beaten
finely grated zest of 1 orange
½ teaspoon almond essence
170 g (6 oz/¾ cup) caster (superfine) sugar

Churros and hot mocha

110 g (3¾ oz/½ cup) raw (demerara) sugar
1 teaspoon ground cinnamon
30 g (1 oz) unsalted butter
125 g (4½ oz/1 cup) plain (all-purpose) flour
½ teaspoon salt
2 eggs
peanut or vegetable oil, for deep frying

Hot mocha
200 g (7 oz) dark chocolate, coarsely grated
750 ml (26 fl oz/3 cups) milk
500 ml (17 fl oz/2 cups) cream
250 ml (9 fl oz/1 cup) freshly made hot
espresso coffee
sugar, to sweeten (optional)

Combine the sugar and cinnamon in a small bowl and set aside.

Place the butter, flour, salt and 250 ml (9 fl oz/1 cup) water in a saucepan over low heat and stir until the mixture is smooth and comes away from the side of the pan. Remove from the heat and add the eggs, one at a time, stirring well after each addition. If the mixture is too soft, return the saucepan to the heat for 1 minute and stir until a little firmer. Spoon the dough into a piping bag fitted with a 5 mm (¼ inch) star nozzle.

Pour the oil into a deep-fryer or a large heavy-based saucepan to a depth of 6 cm (2½ inch) and heat to 190°C (375°F), or until a cube of bread turns golden brown in 10 seconds. Cooking in batches of four or five at a time, pipe 8 cm (3¼ inch) lengths of dough into the oil, snipping off the ends with scissors. Cook for 2–3 minutes, turning once. Use a slotted spoon to transfer the churros to a plate lined with paper towel. Toss the churros in the sugar and cinnamon to coat and place on a serving plate.

Meanwhile, to make the hot mocha, divide the chocolate between six glasses. Place the milk and cream in a saucepan and bring just to the boil. Pour the milk mixture into the glasses, add the coffee and stir to melt the chocolate. Sweeten to taste with sugar, if desired.

Serve the churros with the hot mocha.

Coffee-infused French toast with cherries

Trim the top off each croissant to flatten the surface, then cut in half lengthways into 2.5 cm (1 inch) thick slices.

Place the eggs, sugar, cream and 1 tablespoon of the coffee in a bowl and whisk until well combined.

Melt a little of the butter in a non-stick frying pan over medium heat. Working in batches, dip the croissant slices in the egg mixture, coating both sides and draining off excess. Cook for 1–2 minutes on each side, or until golden brown. Repeat with the remaining butter and croissant slices, keeping the cooked croissants warm.

Meanwhile, heat the maple syrup in a small saucepan over low heat to warm through. Add the cherries and the remaining coffee, cook for 1 minute to heat through, then remove from the heat.

Place two croissant slices on a plate and top with the cherries and maple syrup. Dust with the icing sugar and serve immediately.

VARIATION: The cherries could be substituted with the segments from three oranges.

SERVES 6

3 day-old croissants
3 eggs
1 tablespoon sugar
2½ tablespoons cream
1½ tablespoons freshly made espresso coffee, cooled
20 g (¾ oz) butter
200 ml (7 fl oz) maple syrup
300 g (10½ oz) jar pitted black cherries in syrup, drained
icing (confectioners') sugar, sifted, for dusting

15

Coffee, fruit and nut spiral cookies

MAKES 32

100 g (3½ oz) butter, softened
100 g (3½ oz) cream cheese, softened
125 g (4½ oz/1 cup) plain (all-purpose) flour
1 tablespoon icing (confectioners') sugar
1 egg, lightly beaten

Filling
65 g (2½ oz/⅔ cup) pecans, toasted
2 tablespoons caster (superfine) sugar
85 g (3 oz/⅔ cup) raisins
1 tablespoon mixed peel
2 tablespoons freshly made hot espresso coffee
2 tablespoons apricot jam

Beat the butter and cream cheese in a bowl using electric beaters until well combined. Stir in the flour and sugar to form a dough. Shape the dough into a disc, cover with plastic wrap and refrigerate for 1 hour, or until firm.

Meanwhile, to make the filling, place the pecans and sugar in the bowl of a food processor and pulse until the mixture resembles coarse breadcrumbs. Add the raisins and mixed peel and continue to pulse until roughly chopped. Transfer to a bowl, pour in the coffee and mix well. Set aside for 10 minutes, or until cool and all the liquid has been absorbed.

Roll out the dough on a lightly floured work surface to form a 20 x 40 cm (8 x 16 inch) rectangle. Spread the jam evenly over the dough, then top with a layer of the pecan mixture. Starting from a long side, firmly roll the dough into a Swiss (jelly) roll-style log. Cover with plastic wrap and refrigerate for 1 hour.

Preheat the oven to 180°C (350°F/Gas 4). Line a baking tray with baking paper.

Cut the log into 8 mm (⅜ inch) thick slices. Place the slices, in a single layer, on the prepared tray and brush with a little beaten egg. Bake for 10–12 minutes, or until golden. Transfer to a wire rack to cool completely.

Petite café au lait with vanilla and cinnamon

Combine the milk, ground cinnamon and vanilla bean and seeds in a small saucepan over low–medium heat and bring to the boil, whisking to froth the milk. Remove the vanilla bean. Pour the coffee and milk into two warmed 200 ml (7 fl oz) bowls, add a cinnamon stick and sweeten with sugar, if desired.

SERVES 2

150 ml (5 fl oz) milk
1 teaspoon ground cinnamon
½ vanilla bean, seeds scraped
150 ml (5 fl oz) freshly made hot espresso coffee
2 cinnamon sticks, to garnish
sugar, to taste

19

Apple and coffee tea cakes

MAKES 8

185 g (6½ oz/1½ cups) plain (all-purpose) flour
1 teaspoon ground cinnamon
¼ teaspoon ground allspice
¾ teaspoon baking powder
¾ teaspoon bicarbonate of soda (baking soda)
125 ml (4 fl oz/½ cup) buttermilk
80 ml (2½ fl oz/⅓ cup) freshly made espresso coffee, cooled
185 g (6½ oz/¾ cup) unsalted butter, softened
140 g (5 oz/¾ cup) soft brown sugar
115 g (4 oz/½ cup) caster (superfine) sugar
2 teaspoons finely grated lemon zest
3 eggs
1 granny smith or golden delicious apple, peeled, cored and thinly sliced

Streusel topping
¼ teaspoon ground allspice
45 g (1¾ oz/¼ cup) soft brown sugar
30 g (1 oz/¼ cup) plain (all-purpose) flour
60 g (2¼ oz/½ cup) chopped pecans
45 g (1¾ oz) unsalted butter, chilled and cut into cubes

Preheat the oven to 180°C (350°F/Gas 4). Grease eight 6 x 8 cm (2½ x 3¼ inch) cake tins and line the base and sides of each tin with baking paper.

To make the streusel topping, place the allspice, sugar, flour and pecans in a small bowl and rub in the butter with your fingertips until the mixture resembles coarse breadcrumbs. Set aside.

Sift the flour, spices, baking powder and bicarbonate of soda into a bowl and set aside. Combine the buttermilk and coffee in a separate bowl and set aside.

Cream the butter and sugars in a third bowl using electric beaters until pale and fluffy, then stir in the zest. Add the eggs, one at a time, beating well after each addition. Fold in the flour mixture, alternately with the buttermilk mixture, stirring until just combined and smooth. Stir in the apple slices.

Spoon the batter into the prepared tins and smooth the surface with the back of a spoon. Bake for 10 minutes, then remove from the oven and sprinkle the streusel mixture over the top. Return to the oven for a further 15 minutes or until golden brown and a skewer inserted into the centre of a cake comes out clean. Cool for 10 minutes in the tins before transferring to wire racks to cool completely.

Serve warm or at room temperature.

NOTE: Twelve smaller cakes can be made using 4 x 8 cm (1½ x 3¼ inch) cake tins. Bake for 20 minutes.

Sticky coffee buns

MAKES 24

2 teaspoons dried yeast
2 tablespoons caster (superfine) sugar
150 ml (5 fl oz) tepid milk
75 g (2¾ oz) unsalted butter
340 g (11¾ oz/2¾ cups) plain (all-purpose) flour
½ teaspoon salt
1 egg, lightly beaten
finely grated zest of 1 orange
55 g (2 oz/¼ cup) soft brown sugar
2 teaspoons ground cinnamon

Syrup topping
125 g (4½ oz/½ cup) unsalted butter, melted
115 g (4 oz/½ cup) soft brown sugar
1 teaspoon natural vanilla extract
2 tablespoons freshly made strong espresso coffee

Combine the yeast, a pinch of the caster sugar and 60 ml (2 fl oz/¼ cup) of the milk in a bowl. Set aside for 10 minutes, or until frothy.

Place the butter and the remaining caster sugar and milk in a small saucepan over medium heat and cook, stirring to dissolve the sugar, until the butter is melted. Remove from the heat and set aside to cool until tepid.

Combine the flour and salt in a large bowl and make a well in the centre.

Add the egg, orange zest and the butter mixture to the yeast mixture and stir to combine, then pour into the dry ingredients and stir with a wooden spoon. Continue to mix with your hands until the dough just comes together. Transfer the dough to a lightly floured work surface and knead for 10–12 minutes, or until a smooth, soft dough forms. Place the dough in a lightly greased bowl and cover with plastic wrap. Leave to rise in a warm place for 1 hour, or until doubled in size.

Preheat the oven to 180°C (350°F/Gas 4). Line the base and sides of two 10 x 20 cm (4 x 8 inch) loaf (bar) tins with baking paper.

Meanwhile, prepare the syrup topping. Combine the butter, sugar and vanilla in a bowl and stir in the coffee. Divide the mixture evenly between the prepared tins.

Divide the dough in half. Roll out each portion on a lightly floured work surface to form a 15 x 40 cm (6 x 16 inch) rectangle. Sprinkle the brown sugar and cinnamon over the top. Starting from a long side, firmly roll the dough into Swiss roll (jelly roll)-style logs. Cut each log into 12 spiral slices. Arrange 12 spirals, cut side facing upwards, in each tin. Cover with a tea towel and leave to rise for 30 minutes, or until doubled in size.

Bake for 25–30 minutes, or until golden brown. Invert onto a plate, allowing any excess syrup to drip down the buns. Serve warm.

Almond and coffee meringue hearts

Place the egg whites in a large bowl and beat using electric beaters until stiff peaks form. Gradually add the sugar, a spoonful at a time, and beat until the sugar has dissolved and the meringue mixture is thick and glossy. Whisk in the lemon juice. Remove 150 g (5½ oz/1 cup) of the meringue mixture and set aside.

Combine the lemon zest, ground almonds, cinnamon and coffee in a separate bowl and fold into the meringue mixture to form a thick dough. Refrigerate for 1 hour, or until the dough is firm.

Preheat the oven to 180°C (350°F/Gas 4). Line two baking trays with baking paper.

Dust a clean work surface with the extra sugar and roll out the dough to 8 mm (⅜ inch) thick. Cut the dough into hearts using a lightly greased 5 cm (2 inch) heart-shaped cookie cutter and transfer to the prepared trays. Place teaspoonfuls of the reserved meringue mixture on top of each biscuit shape and spread out evenly using the back of a spoon or a small spatula. Set aside for 15 minutes to dry out the meringue. Bake for 10–12 minutes, or until light golden brown around the edges. Transfer to a wire rack to cool completely.

MAKES 40

3 egg whites
335 g (11¾ oz/2⅔ cups) icing (confectioners') sugar, sifted, plus extra for dusting
½ teaspoon lemon juice
finely grated zest of ½ lemon
200 g (7 oz/2 cups) ground almonds
1 teaspoon ground cinnamon
2 teaspoons finely ground espresso coffee beans

Coconut and pistachio friands with coffee syrup

MAKES 10

150 g (5½ oz/1 cup) pistachio nuts
60 g (2¼ oz/½ cup) plain (all-purpose) flour
155 g (5½ oz/1¼ cups) icing (confectioners') sugar
30 g (1 oz/⅓ cup) desiccated coconut
5 egg whites
185 g (6½ oz/¾ cup) unsalted butter, melted and cooled to room temperature

Coffee syrup
55 g (2 oz/¼ cup) caster (superfine) sugar
1 tablespoon freshly made espresso coffee

To make the coffee syrup, place the sugar, coffee and 1½ tablespoons water in a small saucepan over medium heat and bring to the boil. Simmer for 1–2 minutes, or until the mixture becomes syrupy. Set aside.

Preheat the oven to 190°C (375°F/Gas 5). Grease ten 125 ml (4 fl oz/½ cup) capacity friand tins.

Roughly chop one-third of the pistachios and set aside.

Sift the flour and sugar into a large bowl and set aside. Place the remaining pistachios in the bowl of a food processor and process to fine crumbs. Stir the ground pistachios and coconut into the flour mixture. Whisk the egg whites in a separate bowl until frothy, then stir into the dry ingredients until just combined. Pour in the melted butter and mix well.

Spoon the batter into the prepared tins and sprinkle the reserved chopped pistachios on top. Bake for 20–25 minutes, or until a skewer inserted into the centre of a friand comes out clean. Set aside to cool in the tins for 5 minutes, then turn out onto a wire rack. Place a baking tray under the rack and spoon the warm coffee syrup over the top of the friands. Allow to cool.

Espresso lassi

Place the milk and cardamom pods in a saucepan over medium heat and bring to a simmer for 1 minute. Remove from the heat, set aside to cool, then strain. Pour the infused milk into a plastic container, cover and place in the freezer. Chill until frozen.

Break up the frozen milk and place in a blender, add the yoghurt and half the coffee and blend until slushy. Spoon the lassi into glasses, drizzle in the remaining coffee and dust with the ground cardamom. Stir in some sugar to sweeten to taste, if desired.

SERVES 2–4

500 ml (17 fl oz/2 cups) milk
4 cardamom pods, lightly crushed
90 g (3¼ oz/⅓ cup) Greek-style yoghurt
80 ml (2½ fl oz/⅓ cup) freshly made espresso
  coffee, cooled
ground cardamom, for dusting
sugar, to sweeten (optional)

Nut and coffee breakfast bar

MAKES 25

15 g (½ oz/½ cup) puffed rice
50 g (1¾ oz/½ cup) rolled (porridge) oats
1 tablespoon finely ground espresso coffee beans
25 g (1 oz/¼ cup) ground almonds
60 g (2¼ oz/½ cup) chopped hazelnuts, toasted
70 g (2½ oz/½ cup) pepitas (pumpkin seeds), toasted
90 g (3¼ oz/½ cup) finely chopped dried apricots or pears
60 g (2¼ oz/½ cup) LSA mixture (ground linseeds [flaxseeds], sesame seeds and almonds)
45 g (1¾ oz/½ cup) desiccated coconut
115 g (4 oz/⅓ cup) honey
80 ml (2½ fl oz/⅓ cup) glucose syrup
1 tablespoon sesame seeds
100 g (3½ oz) dark chocolate, melted (optional)

Line a 20 cm (8 inch) square cake tin with baking paper, extending the paper over two opposite sides for easy removal later.

Place the puffed rice, oats, ground coffee, ground almonds, hazelnuts, pepitas, dried fruit, LSA and coconut in a large bowl and mix well. Warm the honey and glucose in a small saucepan over low heat, then pour over the dry ingredients and stir until firm but slightly sticky, adding extra LSA if the mixture is too soft and moist. Spoon the mixture into the prepared tin and smooth the surface, pressing down firmly with the back of a spoon or slightly wet hands. Sprinkle on the sesame seeds, cover with plastic wrap, then place another 20 cm (8 inch) square cake tin on top and weigh down with tinned food. Refrigerate for 3–4 hours, or until firm.

Remove from the tin and cut into 4 cm (1½ inch) squares. Drizzle the chocolate, if desired, over the squares and allow to set. Wrap the individual squares in baking paper and keep refrigerated until required.

These bars will keep, stored in an airtight container in the refrigerator, for up to 5 days.

Baked pears on brioche with coffee mascarpone

Core the pears and slice into 1.5 cm (⅝ inch) rounds. Combine the lemon juice, liqueur and demerara sugar in a bowl. Add the pear slices and set aside to macerate for 15 minutes.

Meanwhile, place the coffee and icing sugar in a bowl and stir to dissolve the sugar. Mix in the mascarpone until just combined. Do not overmix as the mascarpone will become grainy in texture. Cover with plastic wrap and refrigerate until required.

Preheat the oven to 180°C (350°F/Gas 4). Place the pear slices on a baking tray in a single layer, dot a small knob of butter on top and drizzle on the macerating juice. Bake for 20 minutes, or until the pears are tender and golden.

Meanwhile, trim the sides, base and top of the brioche. Cut the brioche into six 2.5 cm (1 inch) thick slices, then shape each slice into a 10 cm (4 inch) round. Toast the brioche until golden brown. Top each slice of brioche with two or three slices of baked pear and drizzle with any pear juices from the tray. Serve with a dollop of the coffee-scented mascarpone.

MAKES 6

3 firm beurre bosc pears
1 tablespoon lemon juice
2 tablespoons Poire William or brandy or orange liqueur
55 g (2 oz/¼ cup) demerara sugar
1 tablespoon freshly made espresso coffee, cooled
2 tablespoons sifted icing (confectioners') sugar
125 g (4½ oz) mascarpone cheese
30 g (1 oz) unsalted butter
450 g (1 lb) brioche loaf

Cinnamon and coffee muffins

MAKES 12

125 g (4½ oz/1 cup) self-raising flour
150 g (5½ oz/1 cup) wholemeal (whole-wheat)
self-raising flour
1½ teaspoons ground cinnamon
115 g (4 oz/½ cup) soft brown sugar
185 ml (6 fl oz/¾ cup) warm milk
2 tablespoons instant coffee granules
2 eggs, lightly beaten
125 g (4½ oz/½ cup) unsalted butter, melted
and cooled

Honey butter
125 g (4½ oz/½ cup) unsalted butter, softened
2 tablespoons honey

Preheat the oven to 190°C (375°F/Gas 5). Grease a 12-hole standard muffin tin.

Sift the flours and cinnamon into a large bowl, adding the leftover husks in the sieve, and stir in the sugar.

Pour the milk into a jug, add the coffee and stir until the coffee has dissolved. Whisk in the eggs and butter, pour into the dry ingredients and stir to just combine—the batter will be slightly lumpy. Spoon into the prepared tin. Bake for 20–25 minutes, or until a skewer inserted into the centre of a muffin comes out clean. Remove from the tin and set aside to cool slightly on a wire rack.

Meanwhile, to make the honey butter, beat the butter and honey in a small bowl until combined and creamy. Transfer to a serving dish.

Serve the muffins warm with the honey butter.

Pecan and coffee sugar cookies

Preheat the oven to 180°C (350°F/Gas 4). Line two baking trays with baking paper.

Combine the icing sugar and ground coffee in a bowl and set aside.

Place the pecans and 1 tablespoon of the caster sugar in the bowl of a food processor and process until the mixture resembles fine breadcrumbs.

Cream the butter and the remaining caster sugar in a large bowl using electric beaters until pale and fluffy. Add the egg yolk and beat until well combined. Stir in the ground pecan mixture, sift in the flour and salt and mix to form a dough.

Roll pieces of the dough into 2.5 cm (1 inch) balls, place on the prepared trays and flatten slightly. Bake for 10 minutes, or until lightly golden around the edges and cooked through. Transfer to a wire rack and, while the cookies are still hot, sift the sugar and coffee mixture over the top. Set aside to cool completely.

MAKES 45

40 g (1½ oz/⅓ cup) icing (confectioners') sugar
1½ tablespoons very finely ground espresso coffee beans
100 g (3½ oz/1 cup) pecans
55 g (2 oz/¼ cup) caster (superfine) sugar
185 g (6½ oz/¾ cup) unsalted butter, softened
1 egg yolk
200 g (7 oz/1⅔ cups) plain (all-purpose) flour
pinch of salt

Apricot ricotta tarts with coffee crème fraîche

MAKES 12

175 g (6 oz) ricotta cheese
125 g (4½ oz/½ cup) unsalted butter, softened
90 g (3¼ oz/½ cup) raw caster (superfine) sugar
3 eggs, separated
finely grated zest and juice of 1 orange
100 g (3½ oz) ground hazelnuts
75 g (2¾ oz) plain (all-purpose) flour
6 firm ripe apricots, halved and stones removed

Coffee crème fraîche
200 g (7 oz) crème fraîche
30 g (1 oz/¼ cup) icing (confectioners') sugar
1 tablespoon freshly made espresso coffee, cooled

To make the coffee crème fraîche, place the crème fraîche in a bowl, sift in the sugar and stir to combine. Mix in the coffee, cover with plastic wrap and place in the refrigerator until required.

Preheat the oven to 180°C (350°F/Gas 4). Grease a 12-hole standard muffin tin and line each base with baking paper.

Use the back of a spoon to push the ricotta through a sieve over a bowl.

Cream the butter and sugar in a bowl using electric beaters until pale and fluffy. Add the egg yolks, one at a time, beating well after each addition. Stir in the ricotta, orange zest and juice, then fold in the combined ground hazelnuts and flour. Beat the egg whites in a separate bowl until stiff peaks form and fold into the ricotta mixture. Spoon the batter into the prepared tin and smooth the surface with the back of a spoon. Place an apricot half, skin side down, on top of the batter. Bake for 12–15 minutes, or until cooked through.

Serve hot with a dollop of the coffee crème fraîche.

VARIATION: Replace the apricots with plums or raspberries.

Semolina pancakes with clotted coffee cream

SERVES 6

65 g (2½ oz/½ cup) fine semolina
155 g (5½ oz/1¼ cups) self-raising flour
2 tablespoons caster (superfine) sugar
3 eggs
375 ml (13 fl oz/1½ cups) milk
1 teaspoon natural vanilla extract
¼ teaspoon freshly grated nutmeg, for dusting

Blueberries in syrup
230 g (8¼ oz/1 cup) caster (superfine) sugar
1 tablespoon lemon juice
250 g (9 oz) blueberries
1 teaspoon orange blossom water (optional)

Clotted coffee cream
250 g (9 oz) clotted cream
1 tablespoon honey
1 tablespoon freshly made hot espresso coffee

To make the blueberries in syrup, combine the sugar, lemon juice and 150 ml (5 fl oz) water in a saucepan over medium heat and stir to dissolve the sugar. Bring to a simmer and cook for 5 minutes, or until syrupy. Add the blueberries and orange blossom water, if using, and simmer for 2 minutes, or until the blueberries are slightly softened. Remove from the heat and set aside to cool to room temperature.

To make the clotted coffee cream, place the cream in a bowl. Combine the honey and coffee in a small bowl, mix well and fold into the cream. Cover and refrigerate until required.

Sift the semolina, flour and sugar into a large bowl and make a well in the centre. Whisk the eggs, milk and vanilla in a separate bowl, then pour into the well. Whisk to form a smooth batter. Set aside for 10 minutes.

Grease a large non-stick frying pan and place over medium–high heat. Add the batter in large spoonfuls and cook, in batches of five or six, for 1–2 minutes, or until bubbles appear on the surface. Flip the pancakes, cook for a further minute, or until golden, and keep warm. Repeat this process with the remaining batter.

Stack three pancakes on each serving plate and spoon the blueberries in syrup over the top. Place a dollop of clotted coffee cream alongside, dust with the nutmeg and serve.

Iced coffee frappé

Pour the coffee into an ice-cube tray and place in the freezer for 2 hours, or until frozen.

Place the coffee ice cubes in a zip-lock bag and hit with a rolling pin until crushed. Reserve one quarter of the crushed ice and transfer the remaining crushed ice to a blender. Add the milk and ice cream, then blend for 30 seconds. Pour into two serving glasses and serve immediately, topped with the reserved crushed ice.

SERVES 2

250 ml (9 fl oz/1 cup) freshly made strong
   espresso coffee, cooled
375 ml (13 fl oz/1½ cups) milk
2 scoops vanilla ice cream

Hazelnut and espresso shortbread

MAKES 80

200 g (7 oz/1⅔ cups) plain (all-purpose) flour
2 tablespoons finely ground espresso
coffee beans
90 g (3¼ oz) caster (superfine) sugar, plus extra
for dusting
160 g (5¾ oz/⅔ cup) unsalted butter, chilled and
cut into cubes
55 g (2 oz/½ cup) ground hazelnuts
icing (confectioners') sugar, sifted, for dusting

Sift the flour and ground coffee into a large bowl, add the caster sugar and stir to combine. Rub the butter into the dry ingredients with your fingertips until the mixture resembles coarse breadcrumbs. Add the ground hazelnuts, then, working quickly, use your hands to mix and form a dough. Shape into a disc, cover with plastic wrap and refrigerate for 30 minutes.

Preheat the oven to 180°C (350°F/Gas 4). Line two baking trays with baking paper.

Knead the dough for 2 minutes, then roll out between two sheets of baking paper to 1 cm (½ inch) thick. Cut the dough into flower shapes using a 2.5 cm (1 inch) flower-shaped cookie cutter, re-rolling the remaining dough and cutting out more shapes until all the dough is used. Transfer to the prepared trays. Place in the refrigerator for 20 minutes.

Dust the tops of the biscuits with the extra caster sugar and bake for 10–12 minutes, or until lightly golden around the edges. Dust with the icing sugar while hot and set aside to cool completely on the trays.

Bombolini with mocha cream

Place the milk and yeast in a bowl, stir well and set aside for 10 minutes, or until frothy.

Combine the flour, caster sugar and salt in a large bowl and make a well in the centre. Add the egg, lemon zest, butter and yeast mixture and stir until incorporated. Transfer to a lightly floured work surface and knead for 8–10 minutes, or until a smooth dough forms. Place the dough in a lightly greased bowl and set aside in a warm place for 1 hour, or until doubled in size.

Line two baking trays with baking paper. Divide the dough in half. Roll out each portion on a lightly floured work surface to 2 cm (¾ inch) thick. Cut the dough into rounds using a 4.5 cm (1¾ inch) cookie cutter. Transfer to the prepared trays, leaving room for spreading. Cover loosely and rest in a warm place for 1 hour, or until doubled in size.

Meanwhile, make the mocha cream. Place the cream and chocolate in a heatproof bowl over a saucepan of simmering water, making sure the bowl doesn't touch the water. Cook, stirring, until the chocolate has melted. Remove from the heat, add the coffee and stir until the coffee has dissolved. Set aside to cool.

Spread the raw caster sugar on a plate. Pour the oil into a deep-fryer or a large heavy-based saucepan to a depth of 5 cm (2 inches) and heat to 180°C (350°F), or until a piece of the dough sizzles when it hits the hot oil. Cook the rounds, in batches, for 1 minute on each side, or until golden. Drain on paper towel. Toss the bombolini in the raw caster sugar. Serve warm, dipped in the mocha cream.

MAKES 20

125 ml (4 fl oz/½ cup) tepid milk
4 teaspoons dried yeast
250 g (9 oz/2 cups) plain (all-purpose) flour
2 tablespoons caster (superfine) sugar
pinch of salt
1 egg
1 teaspoon finely grated lemon zest
25 g (1 oz) unsalted butter, softened
90 g (3¼ oz/½ cup) raw caster (superfine) sugar, for dusting
vegetable oil, for deep frying

Mocha cream
80 ml (2½ fl oz/⅓ cup) cream
200 g (7 oz) white chocolate, chopped
1 tablespoon instant coffee granules

Sugar hits

Get your afternoon caffeine fix with these
tempting tidbits.

Meringue kisses with chocolate coffee cream

MAKES 20

2 egg whites
¼ teaspoon almond essence
115 g (4 oz/½ cup) caster (superfine) sugar

Chocolate coffee cream
200 g (7 oz) dark chocolate, chopped
1 tablespoon instant coffee granules
125 ml (4 fl oz/½ cup) cream (whipping)

Preheat the oven to 150°C (300°F/Gas 2). Line two baking trays with baking paper.

Place the egg whites in a large bowl and beat using electric beaters until firm peaks form. Mix in the almond essence, then add the sugar, a spoonful at a time, and beat until the sugar has dissolved and the mixture is thick and glossy. Transfer the meringue mixture to a piping (icing) bag fitted with a 1 cm (½ inch) plain nozzle and pipe rounds at 3 cm (1¼ inch) intervals, allowing room for spreading, onto the prepared trays. Alternatively, place teaspoons of the meringue mixture, spacing them well apart, on the prepared trays. Bake for 45 minutes. Turn off the oven and leave the door slightly ajar, allowing the meringues to cool slowly.

To make the chocolate coffee cream, place the chocolate, coffee and cream in a heatproof bowl over a saucepan of simmering water, ensuring the bowl doesn't touch the water. Stir until the chocolate has melted and the mixture is smooth. Cool, cover with plastic wrap and refrigerate until required.

Use the chocolate coffee cream to sandwich the meringues together.

These filled meringues are best eaten immediately. Unfilled meringues will keep, stored in an airtight container, for up to 2 weeks.

Sugar and spice coffee

Place the cloves, cinnamon, lemon zest, sugar and 700 ml (24 fl oz) water in a saucepan over medium heat and bring to the boil. Stir in the ground coffee, reduce the heat to low and simmer for 5 minutes. Strain through a coffee filter or a muslin-lined sieve into a jug. Divide between four tall glasses and add in the Kahlua. Place a spoonful of cream on top and dust with the nutmeg.

SERVES 4

6 whole cloves
1 cinnamon stick
1 strip lemon zest, white pith removed
55 g (2 oz/¼ cup) dark brown sugar
25 g (1 oz/⅓ cup) finely ground espresso coffee beans
2 tablespoons Kahlua
80 ml (2½ fl oz/⅓ cup) cream, lightly whipped
freshly grated nutmeg, to sprinkle

Sour cream and coffee walnut cakes

MAKES 10

60 g (2¼ oz/⅓ cup) soft brown sugar
75 g (2¾ oz/¾ cup) walnut halves
1 teaspoon finely ground espresso coffee beans
1 teaspoon ground cinnamon
115 g (4 oz) unsalted butter, softened
115 g (4 oz/½ cup) caster (superfine) sugar
2 eggs
185 g (6½ oz/1½ cups) plain (all-purpose) flour
¾ teaspoon baking powder
½ teaspoon bicarbonate of soda (baking soda)
225 g (8 oz) sour cream
10 walnut halves, to decorate

Icing
155 g (5½ oz/1¼ cups) icing (confectioners')
sugar, sifted
2–3 teaspoons freshly made strong
espresso coffee

Preheat the oven to 180°C (350°F/Gas 4). Grease 10 friand tins and line the bases with baking paper.

Place the brown sugar, walnuts, ground coffee and cinnamon in the bowl of a food processor and pulse until the mixture resembles coarse breadcrumbs. Add 40 g (1½ oz) of the butter and process until well combined. Set aside.

Cream the remaining butter and the caster sugar in a bowl using electric beaters until pale and fluffy. Add the eggs, one at a time, beating well after each addition. Sift the flour, baking powder and bicarbonate of soda into a separate bowl. Stir one-third of the flour mixture, then one-third of the sour cream, into the egg mixture, and continue alternating until all the flour mixture and sour cream is incorporated and well combined.

Spoon half the batter into the prepared tins and spread across the base. Sprinkle the reserved walnut mixture over the batter, then spoon on the remaining batter to cover evenly. Bake for 20–25 minutes, or until lightly golden and a skewer inserted into the centre of a cake comes out clean. Set aside to cool slightly in the tins, then turn out onto a wire rack to cool completely.

To make the icing, place the sugar in a bowl and stir in enough coffee, adding a little water if necessary, to make a smooth, spreadable consistency.

Spread the icing over the cakes and place a walnut half on top. Allow icing to cool before serving.

Coffee and nut brittle

MAKES 24

500 g (1 lb 2 oz) sugar
90 g (3¼ oz/¼ cup) honey
60 g (2¼ oz/¼ cup) unsalted butter
170 ml (5½ fl oz/⅔ cup) freshly made strong espresso coffee, cooled
½ teaspoon bicarbonate of soda (baking soda)
1 teaspoon natural vanilla extract
80 g (2¾ oz/½ cup) whole almonds, toasted
70 g (2½ oz/½ cup) pistachio nuts, toasted
80 g (2¾ oz/½ cup) unsalted peanuts or cashews, toasted

Line a baking tray with baking paper.

Combine the sugar, honey, butter and coffee in a heavy-based saucepan over medium heat and stir to dissolve the sugar. Continue to cook, without stirring, until the mixture reaches hard crack stage (a little of the syrup dropped into a bowl of cold water forms hard brittle threads that break when bent), or 150°C (300°F) on a sugar (candy) thermometer. Remove from the heat and, working quickly before the mixture hardens, stir in the bicarbonate of soda, vanilla and nuts. Pour onto the prepared tray and smooth the surface with a greased spatula. Cool at room temperature until set hard.

When set, break the brittle into large shards to serve.

Honey-spiced coffee madeleines

Preheat the oven to 190°C (375°F/Gas 5)
Grease 36 madeleine moulds.

Beat the eggs and caster sugar in a large bowl using electric beaters until pale and creamy. Sift together the flour, baking powder, ground coffee and spices and gently fold into the egg mixture. Combine the honey and butter in a small bowl and fold into the batter. Divide the batter evenly among the prepared moulds. Bake for 7–10 minutes, or until golden and springy to touch. Allow the madeleines to cool in the moulds for 1 minute, then turn out onto a wire rack to cool completely.

Arrange the madeleines on a serving plate and dust with the icing sugar.

Madeleines are best eaten on the day they are made.

MAKES 36

2 eggs
55 g (2 oz/¼ cup) caster (superfine) sugar
60 g (2¼ oz/½ cup) plain (all-purpose) flour
pinch of baking powder
1 teaspoon finely ground espresso coffee beans
pinch of freshly grated nutmeg
¼ teaspoon mixed (pumpkin pie) spice
1 tablespoon honey
60 g (2¼ oz) unsalted butter, melted
icing (confectioners') sugar, sifted, for dusting

Sticky nut and coffee pastries

MAKES 36

125 g (4½ oz/1¼ cups) walnut halves
115 g (4 oz/¾ cup) whole almonds
12 sheets filo pastry
150 g (5½ oz) unsalted butter, melted
110 g (3¾ oz/⅔ cup) pistachio nuts, lightly
toasted and coarsely chopped
sheep's milk yoghurt (optional)

Syrup
2 cinnamon sticks
6 cardamom pods, lightly crushed
finely grated zest of 1 orange
juice of 2 oranges
450 g (1 lb/2 cups) caster (superfine) sugar
235 g (8½ oz/⅔ cup) honey
170 ml (5½ fl oz/⅔ cup) freshly made strong hot
espresso or Greek coffee

To make the syrup, combine the cinnamon, cardamom, orange zest and juice, sugar, honey, coffee and 250 ml (9 fl oz/1 cup) water in a saucepan over medium heat and stir to dissolve the sugar. Bring to a simmer and cook, without stirring, for 10 minutes, or until the syrup begins to thicken. Set aside to cool, remove and discard the spices.

Preheat the oven to 170°C (325°F/Gas 3). Line a baking tray with baking paper.

Spread the walnuts and almonds on the prepared tray. Toast for 5–8 minutes, or until lightly golden. Finely chop and set aside.

Place a sheet of filo on a work surface. Keep the remaining filo sheets covered with a damp tea towel (dish towel). Brush the filo sheet with a little of the melted butter. Cover with another sheet of filo and brush with some of the remaining melted butter. Sprinkle one-sixth, about 40 g (1½ oz), of the chopped walnuts and almonds over the pastry, leaving a 2 cm (¾ inch) border at one end. Starting at the opposite end roll up the pastry like a Swiss (jelly) roll-style, brushing with melted butter at every turn. Transfer the roll to the prepared tray. Repeat this process with the remaining pastry, melted butter and walnuts and almonds.

Bake for 15 minutes, reduce the temperature to 150°C (300°F/Gas 2) and bake for a further 10 minutes, or until golden brown. Allow to cool on the tray. Trim the ends, cut each roll into three 8 cm (3¼ inch) lengths, then cut in half on the diagonal. Transfer to a ceramic dish and pour on the syrup. Cover with plastic wrap and set aside to soak overnight in a cool place.

Dip the diagonally cut ends in the chopped pistachios and arrange, standing upright, on a serving plate. Serve with the yoghurt, if desired.

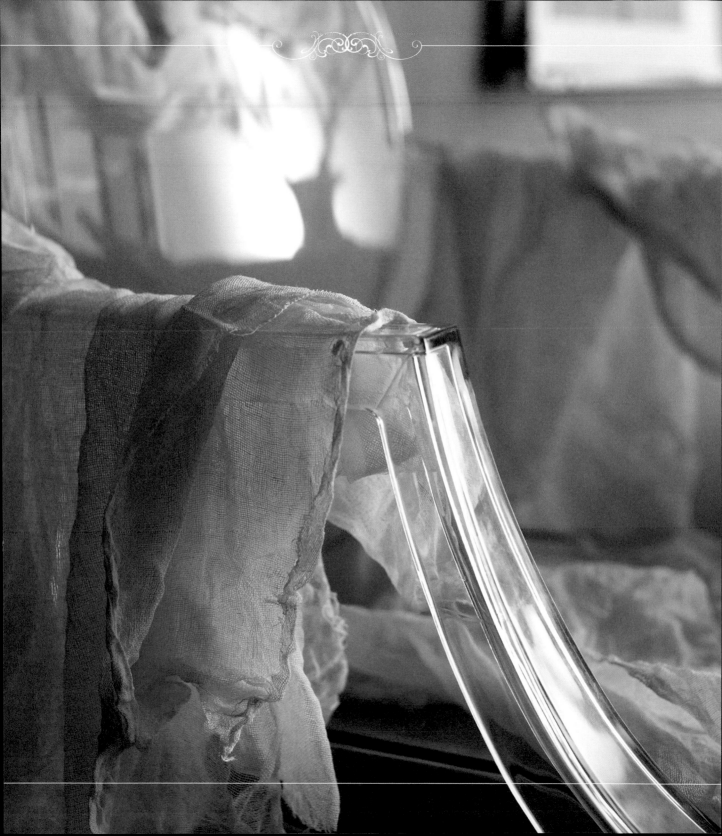

Iced coffee with a Vietnamese twist

SERVES 4

1 tablespoon sugar
125 ml (4 fl oz/½ cup) freshly made hot
espresso coffee
2 teaspoons powdered gelatine
105 g (3½ oz/⅓ cup) condensed milk
125 ml (4 fl oz/½ cup) coconut milk
135 g (4¾ oz/1 cup) ice, crushed
300 ml (10½ fl oz) freshly made espresso
coffee, chilled

Place the sugar, hot coffee and 125 ml (4 fl oz/½ cup) water in a small saucepan over low heat. Add the gelatine and stir to dissolve. Remove from the heat and pour into a 10 x 14 cm (4 x 5½ inch) shallow tray. Place in the refrigerator for 30 minutes, or until set.

Cut the jelly into shreds and divide among four 200 ml (7 fl oz) glasses. Place 1 tablespoon of condensed milk on the jelly, then add 1½ tablespoons of coconut milk. Top with the crushed ice and pour on the chilled coffee. Serve with a spoon.

Amaretti with a hint of espresso

Preheat the oven to 220°C (425°F/Gas 7). Line a baking tray with baking paper.

Combine the ground almonds, icing sugar and ground coffee in a bowl and stir to mix well. Whisk the egg white in a separate bowl until frothy, then gradually stir into the dry ingredients to form a firm dough.

Transfer the dough to a lightly floured surface and roll into a 30 cm (12 inch) log shape. Cut into 1 cm (½ inch) slices, then shape each slice into a ball and coat in the caster sugar. Place on the prepared tray, allowing room for spreading, and bake for 8–10 minutes, or until pale brown. Leave to cool on the tray. The amaretti will become crisp as they cool.

MAKES 30

100 g (3½ oz/1 cup) ground almonds
125 g (4½ oz/1 cup) icing (confectioners') sugar, sifted
1 teaspoon finely ground espresso coffee beans
1 egg white
55 g (2 oz/¼ cup) caster (superfine) sugar

Coffee caramel tartlets

MAKES 24

75 g (2¾ oz) unsalted butter, softened
50 g (1¾ oz) icing (confectioners') sugar
1 egg yolk
30 g (1 oz/¼ cup) ground hazelnuts
125 g (4½ oz/1 cup) plain (all-purpose) flour
24 assorted chocolate-coated coffee beans

Coffee caramel cream
20 g (¾ oz/¼ cup) finely ground espresso
coffee beans
80 cm (31½ inch) square piece muslin
185 ml (6 fl oz/¾ cup) cream
75 g (2¾ oz) unsalted butter
170 g (6 oz/¾ cup) caster (superfine) sugar

Place the butter and sugar in the bowl of a food processor and pulse until just creamy. Add the egg yolk and ground hazelnuts and process to mix well. Add the flour and pulse until the dough just comes together. Shape the dough into a disc, cover with plastic wrap and refrigerate for at least 1 hour.

Preheat the oven to 180°C (350°F/Gas 4). Lightly grease two 12-hole mini muffin tins.

Roll out the pastry between two pieces of baking paper to 2 mm (¹⁄₁₆ inch) thick. Cut out rounds using a 6 cm (2½ inch) cookie cutter, re-rolling any off-cuts. Line the prepared tins with the pastry rounds and place in the freezer for 20 minutes. Trim any excess pastry and line each tartlet case with foil. Bake for 10 minutes, or until the pastry is dry. If the pastry has puffed up, gently press down with the fingertips to remove any bubbles. Remove the foil and return the tins to the oven for 5 minutes, or until the pastry is golden and cooked through. Allow the tartlet cases to cool in the tins for 2 minutes, then carefully remove and transfer to a wire rack to cool completely.

To make the coffee caramel cream, place the ground coffee on the triple-folded muslin and tie with kitchen string to secure. Place the cream, butter and muslin-bound coffee in a small saucepan over low heat and cook, stirring occasionally, until the butter melts. Remove from the heat and set aside for 5 minutes to allow the coffee to infuse. Reheat over low heat, remove the muslin bag, squeeze to extract as much liquid as possible, then discard. Meanwhile, place the sugar in a small heavy-based saucepan over medium–low heat and cook, swirling the pan and brushing down the side with a pastry brush dipped in water, until the sugar dissolves and the caramel is golden. Immediately remove from the heat and pour in the hot coffee-infused cream, whisking to dissolve the caramel. Strain into a small bowl, cover with plastic wrap and refrigerate for 1 hour.

Fill each tartlet case with a teaspoon of the coffee caramel cream and top with a chocolate-coated coffee bean. Allow to cool.

Hazelnut cakes with coffee cream and muscatel syrup

MAKES 12

45 g (1¾ oz/⅓ cup) hazelnuts, toasted
and skinned
230 g (8¼ oz/1 cup) caster (superfine) sugar
125 g (4½ oz/1 cup) self-raising flour
30 g (1 oz/¼ cup) unsweetened cocoa powder
250 ml (9 fl oz/1 cup) milk
60 g (2¼ oz/¼ cup) unsalted butter, softened
2 eggs, lightly beaten
2 teaspoons finely grated orange zest

Syrup
75 g (2¾ oz) dried muscatels
2 tablespoons amaretto
80 ml (2½ fl oz/⅓ cup) freshly made strong
espresso coffee
80 g (2¾ oz/⅓ cup) caster (superfine) sugar

Coffee cream
100 g (3½ oz) unsalted butter, softened
200 g (7 oz) icing (confectioners') sugar, sifted
1½ tablespoons freshly made espresso
coffee, cooled

Preheat the oven to 180°C (350°F/Gas 4). Lightly grease twelve 125 ml (4 fl oz/½ cup) dariole moulds and line the bases with baking paper.

Combine the hazelnuts and sugar in the bowl of a food processor and process until finely ground. Sift the flour and cocoa into a large bowl, add the milk, butter, eggs, orange zest and the hazelnut mixture and beat using electric beaters until fluffy. Spoon the batter into the prepared moulds. Bake for 20–25 minutes, or until just cooked and a skewer inserted into the centre of a cake comes out clean. Allow to cool in the moulds for 5 minutes, then turn out onto a wire rack to cool.

Meanwhile, prepare the syrup. Place the muscatels, amaretto, coffee and sugar in a small saucepan over medium heat and bring to the boil, stirring to dissolve the sugar. Simmer, without stirring, for 5–7 minutes, or until slightly reduced and syrupy. Remove from the heat and set aside to cool.

For the coffee cream, beat the butter, sugar and coffee in a bowl using electric beaters until pale and fluffy.

Spread the coffee cream on the top of each cake, then transfer to a serving plate. Strain the syrup into a bowl, reserving the muscatels. Decorate each cake with the reserved muscatels, spoon a little of the syrup over the top and serve.

Hazelnut cakes without icing will keep, stored in an airtight container, for up to 3 days.

Coffee sponge sandwiches

Preheat the oven to 200°C (400°F/Gas 6). Line two baking trays with baking paper.

Place the eggs, caster sugar and coffee in a large bowl and beat using electric beaters until pale, creamy and doubled in volume. Sift in the flour, cornflour and baking powder and mix well. Place teaspoons of the batter, allowing room for spreading, onto the prepared trays. Bake for 5–6 minutes, or until puffed and lightly golden. Remove the biscuits with a spatula and place on a wire rack to cool completely.

Meanwhile, prepare the filling. Whisk the cream in a large bowl until firm peaks form, then gently swirl in the jam.

Use the filling to sandwich the biscuits together, then dust with the icing sugar and serve.

Coffee sponge sandwiches are best filled no longer than 1 hour before serving.

MAKES 24

2 eggs
80 g (2¾ oz/⅓ cup) caster (superfine) sugar
1 teaspoon instant coffee granules
40 g (1½ oz/⅓ cup) self-raising flour
2 tablespoons cornflour (cornstarch)
½ teaspoon baking powder
icing (confectioners') sugar, sifted, for dusting

Filling
250 ml (9 fl oz/1 cup) whipping cream
105 g (3¾ oz/⅓ cup) blackberry jam

Viennese coffee

SERVES 4

250 ml (9 fl oz/1 cup) whipping cream
120 g (4¼ oz) dark chocolate, chopped
600 ml (21 fl oz) freshly made hot
espresso coffee
finely grated dark chocolate, to serve

Beat 185 ml (6 fl oz/¾ cup) of the cream in a small bowl using electric beaters until soft peaks form.

Place the chopped chocolate and the remaining cream in a saucepan over low heat and stir constantly until the chocolate has melted. Pour in the coffee and mix well. Divide among four 185 ml (6 fl oz/¾ cup) serving cups or glasses and spoon the whipped cream on top. Sprinkle on the grated chocolate and serve.

Mini spiced ginger coffee cakes

MAKES 36

1 teaspoon finely ground espresso coffee beans
100 g (3½ oz) fresh dates, pitted and chopped
¼ teaspoon bicarbonate of soda (baking soda)
1 egg
60 ml (2 fl oz/¼ cup) vegetable or light olive oil
80 g (2¾ oz/⅓ cup) soft brown sugar
150 g (5½ oz) treacle (molasses)
1 tablespoon bourbon or dark rum
1 tablespoon glacé (candied) ginger,
finely chopped
155 g (5½ oz/1¼ cups) plain (all-purpose) flour
1 tablespoon unsweetened cocoa powder
½ teaspoon baking powder
½ teaspoon ground cardamom
2 teaspoons ground ginger
icing (confectioners') sugar, sifted, for dusting
4 pieces glacé (candied) ginger, cut into very
fine slivers

Preheat the oven to 180°C (350°F/Gas 4). Grease three 12-hole mini muffin tins and lightly dust with flour.

Place the ground coffee, dates and 185 ml (6 fl oz/¾ cup) water in a small saucepan over medium–high heat, bring to the boil and stir in the bicarbonate of soda. Remove from the heat and cool to lukewarm.

Meanwhile, place the egg, oil, brown sugar, treacle, bourbon or rum and chopped glacé ginger in a large bowl and mix well. Sift in the flour, cocoa, baking powder and spices, stir to combine (the mixture will be very thick), then stir in the date mixture. Spoon the batter into the prepared tins. Bake for 12–15 minutes, or until a skewer inserted in the centre of a cake comes out clean. Allow the cakes to cool in the tins for 5 minutes before turning out onto a wire rack to cool completely.

Dust the cakes with the icing sugar and serve with a sliver of glacé ginger on top.

The cakes will keep, stored in an airtight container, for up to 1 week.

VARIATION: To make small cakes, use twelve 125 ml (4 fl oz/½ cup) capacity dariole moulds and bake for approximately 20–25 minutes.

Coffee bean panforte

Preheat the oven to 150°C (300°F/Gas 2). Lightly brush a 20 cm (8 inch) square cake tin with olive oil. Line the base with the rice paper.

Place the glacé orange, dried figs, nuts and coffee beans in a large heatproof bowl. Sift in the flour, cocoa and spices and stir to combine.

Place the honey and sugar in a small heavy-based saucepan over low heat and stir to dissolve the sugar. Bring to the boil, then reduce the heat to low and continue to cook, without stirring, until the syrup reaches soft ball stage (the mixture should be soft and pliable when dropped into cold water and pressed between your finger and thumb), or 120°C (250°F) on a sugar (candy) thermometer. Carefully pour the syrup over the dry ingredients and, working quickly, stir well before the mixture hardens. Transfer the mixture to the prepared tin and press down firmly with the back of a spoon to spread out and flatten. Bake for 30 minutes. Unlike other cakes this will neither firm up nor colour as it cooks, so you need to time it carefully. Allow the panforte to cool in the tin.

Turn out onto a cutting board and, using a hot knife, cut across the panforte to form three rectangles, then cut each rectangle into four pieces. Halve each piece diagonally to make two triangles. Dust the pieces heavily with the cocoa before serving.

Coffee bean panforte can be stored, wrapped in foil and refrigerated, for up to 6 weeks.

MAKES 24

1 sheet rice paper
100 g (3½ oz) glacé (candied) orange, chopped into small dice
100 g (3½ oz) dried dessert figs, chopped
80 g (2¾ oz/½ cup) whole almonds, toasted
70 g (2½ oz/½ cup) hazelnuts, toasted and skinned
80 g (2¾ oz/½ cup) chocolate-coated coffee beans, roughly chopped
40 g (1½ oz/⅓ cup) plain (all-purpose) flour
2 teaspoons unsweetened cocoa powder
1½ teaspoons ground cinnamon
1 teaspoon mixed spice
90 g (3¼ oz/¼ cup) honey
80 g (2¾ oz/⅓ cup) caster (superfine) sugar
unsweetened cocoa powder, sifted, for dusting

Café choux puffs

100 g (3½ oz) unsalted butter
2 teaspoons caster (superfine) sugar
125 g (4½ oz/1 cup) plain (all-purpose) flour
4 eggs
1 egg beaten with a little water, for glazing
icing (confectioners') sugar, sifted, for dusting

Coffee custard
4 egg yolks
55 g (2 oz/¼ cup) caster (superfine) sugar
2 tablespoons plain (all-purpose) flour
250 ml (9 fl oz/1 cup) milk
200 ml (7 fl oz) thick (double/heavy) cream
1 tablespoon freshly made strong
espresso coffee
½ teaspoon natural vanilla extract

To make the coffee custard, beat the egg yolks and sugar in a bowl until pale and thick, then stir in the flour. Bring the milk, cream and coffee to scalding point in a saucepan over medium heat. Remove from the heat and gradually whisk the milk mixture into the egg mixture. Return the mixture to the clean saucepan, place over low heat and whisk until the custard just comes to the boil and thickens. Remove from the heat and whisk in the vanilla. Transfer to a bowl to cool, cover with plastic wrap and refrigerate until required.

Preheat the oven to 220°C (425°F/Gas 7). Line two baking trays with baking paper.

Place the butter, caster sugar and 250 ml (9 fl oz/1 cup) water in a saucepan over medium heat and bring to the boil. Remove from the heat, add the flour and stir until smooth. Return to the heat and stir for 1–2 minutes, or until the dough pulls away from the side of the pan and forms a ball around the spoon. Remove from the heat. Add the eggs, one at a time, beating well after each addition.

Transfer the choux mixture to a piping (icing) bag fitted with a 1 cm (½ inch) plain nozzle. Pipe 5 cm (2 inch) rounds onto the prepared trays and brush with the egg glaze. Bake for 15 minutes, then reduce the oven temperature to 180°C (350°F/Gas 4) and bake for a further 10 minutes, or until crisp. Transfer to a wire rack, then slice the choux puffs in half to cool.

Fill the choux puffs with the coffee custard, dust with the icing sugar and serve.

Coffee swirl cheesecakes

Line a 12-hole standard muffin tin with paper cases. Preheat the oven to 130°C (250°F/Gas 1).

To make the base, place the biscuits in the bowl of a food processor and process to fine crumbs. Add the butter and pulse to combine. Divide the base mixture among the paper cases and press down firmly with a spoon. Place in the freezer for 10 minutes, or until firm.

Meanwhile, beat the sugar and cream cheese in a large bowl using electric beaters until smooth. Add the eggs and egg yolks, one at a time, beating well after each addition, then stir in the sour cream and coffee. Sift in the flour and stir until just combined. Transfer 125 ml (4 fl oz/½ cup) of the filling to a small bowl, then spoon the remaining filling evenly over the base in the paper cases.

Add the melted chocolate and Kahlua to the reserved filling and mix well. Drop teaspoons of the chocolate mixture on top of the filling and swirl using a wooden skewer. Bake for 30–35 minutes, or until just firm. Allow to cool to room temperature in the tin, then remove and serve.

Coffee swirl cheesecakes will keep, stored in an airtight container in the refrigerator, for up to 3 days.

MAKES 12

150 g (5½ oz) caster (superfine) sugar
500 g (1 lb 2 oz/2 cups) cream cheese, softened
3 eggs
2 egg yolks
140 g (5 oz) sour cream
60 ml (2 fl oz/¼ cup) freshly made strong espresso coffee, cooled
2 tablespoons plain (all-purpose) flour
75 g (2¾ oz) dark chocolate, melted and cooled
2 tablespoons Kahlua

Base
250 g (9 oz) chocolate ripple or plain chocolate biscuits (cookies), broken into pieces
100 g (3½ oz) unsalted butter, melted

Sugar hits

Macadamia brownies with coffee custard

MAKES 16

125 g (4½ oz/½ cup) unsalted butter
200 g (7 oz) dark chocolate, chopped
3 eggs
150 g (5½ oz) demerara sugar
100 g (3½ oz) plain (all-purpose) flour
100 g (3½ oz/¾ cup) macadamia nuts, chopped
sweetened cocoa powder, sifted, for dusting

Coffee custard

2 egg yolks
1½ tablespoons caster (superfine) sugar
2 teaspoons freshly made strong espresso coffee
150 ml (5 fl oz) cream (whipping)
½ vanilla bean, seeds scraped
110 g (3¾ oz/½ cup) mascarpone cheese

Preheat the oven to 180°C (350°F/Gas 4). Line a 20 cm (8 inch) square cake tin with baking paper, extending the paper over the two sides for easy removal later.

Combine the butter and chocolate in a heatproof bowl over a saucepan of simmering water, ensuring the bowl doesn't touch the water. Stir until the butter and chocolate have melted. Remove from the heat and cool.

Beat the eggs and sugar in a bowl using electric beaters until pale and creamy. Fold in the flour until just combined, then fold in the chocolate mixture and the nuts. Pour into the prepared tin. Bake for 25–30 minutes, or until a skewer inserted into the centre comes out with moist crumbs attached. Allow to cool in the tin.

Meanwhile, prepare the coffee custard. Beat the egg yolks and sugar in a large bowl using electric beaters until pale and thick, then stir in the coffee. Place the cream and vanilla bean and seeds in a small saucepan over medium heat and bring to scalding point. Gradually whisk the hot cream into the egg yolk mixture. Return the mixture to the clean saucepan and stir over low heat until the custard coats the back of a wooden spoon. Transfer to a bowl to cool. Cover with plastic wrap and chill. Whisk in the mascarpone and transfer to a serving bowl.

Cut the brownie into 5 cm (2 inch) squares, dust with the cocoa and serve with the coffee custard.

Honey and nut tarts with coffee cream

Cream the butter and sugar in a bowl using electric beaters until pale and fluffy. Sift in the flour and stir to form a soft dough. Divide the dough in half, shape into two discs and cover with plastic wrap. Chill for 1 hour.

Preheat the oven to 180°C (350°F/Gas 4).

Roll out each portion of dough between two pieces of baking paper to 3 mm (⅛ inch) thick. Use the pastry to line twelve 5 cm (2 inch) fluted loose-based tart (flan) tins, trimming excess pastry. Freeze for 20 minutes. Line each tart case with foil, fill with baking weights or uncooked rice and blind bake for 12 minutes. Remove the foil and weights, return to the oven for 5 minutes, or until lightly golden. Cool in the tins.

To make the coffee cream, beat the cream and sugar in a bowl using electric beaters until soft peaks form. Fold in the coffee, cover and chill.

To make the filling, place the cream, honey, sugar and butter in a small saucepan over medium heat and bring to scalding point. Reduce the heat to low and simmer for 1 minute. Remove from the heat and stir in the nuts. Spoon the filling into the tart cases. Bake for 15–20 minutes, or until the cream is bubbling around the edges. Cool in the tins.

Serve the tarts with the coffee cream.

MAKES 12

100 g (3½ oz) unsalted butter, softened
55 g (2 oz/¼ cup) caster (superfine) sugar
150 g (5½ oz) plain (all-purpose) flour

Coffee cream
300 ml (10½ fl oz) whipping cream
1 tablespoon icing (confectioners') sugar
1 tablespoon freshly made strong espresso coffee, chilled

Filling
125 ml (4 fl oz/½ cup) cream
2 tablespoons honey
1 tablespoon caster (superfine) sugar
15 g (½ oz) unsalted butter
270 g (9½ oz/2 cups) mixed slivered almonds, macadamia nuts, pecans and hazelnuts, roughly chopped

Mini double espresso roulade

MAKES 18

100 g (3½ oz) dark chocolate, chopped
2 teaspoons very finely ground espresso
coffee beans
3 eggs, at room temperature, separated
75 g (2¾ oz/⅓ cup) caster (superfine) sugar
2 tablespoons plain (all-purpose) flour
2 tablespoons ground almonds
sweetened cocoa powder, sifted, for dusting

Filling
250 ml (9 fl oz/1 cup) thickened
(whipping) cream
1 tablespoon icing (confectioners') sugar
2 teaspoons very finely ground espresso
coffee beans

Preheat the oven to 180°C (350°F/Gas 4). Grease two 16 x 26 cm (6¼ x 10½ inch) baking tins and line the base of each tin with baking paper, extending the paper over the long sides for easy removal later.

Place the chocolate, coffee and 1½ tablespoons warm water in a heatproof bowl over a saucepan of simmering water, ensuring the bowl doesn't touch the water. Stir until the chocolate has melted. Set aside to cool.

Meanwhile, place the egg yolks and sugar in a large bowl and beat with electric beaters until pale and thick. Gently fold in the chocolate mixture. Beat the egg whites in a separate large bowl using electric beaters until soft peaks form. Fold a large spoonful of the whites into the egg yolk mixture, then fold in the remaining egg whites, and the flour and almonds. Divide the mixture between the prepared tins and spread evenly. Bake for 7–8 minutes, or until a skewer inserted in the centre of a cake comes out clean. Cover the cakes with a sheet of baking paper and a clean damp tea towel (dish towel) and set aside to cool.

To make the filling, whip the cream, sugar and coffee in a bowl using electric beaters until soft peaks form.

Dust two sheets of baking paper with the cocoa. Invert the cakes onto the dusted paper and remove the lining paper. Cut each rectangle crossways into three, to make six 8.5 x 16 cm (3¼ x 6¼ inch) rectangles. Spread on the filling, then gently roll up from a short side, using the paper as a guide. Refrigerate for an hour. Slice each roulade into three and serve dusted with more cocoa.

Dark stars

The nightcap just got sexier with these black gold-laced evening delicacies.

Strawberries in vin santo with ricotta cream

SERVES 6

250 ml (9 fl oz/1 cup) vin santo
55 g (2 oz/¼ cup) soft brown sugar
1½ tablespoons freshly made strong espresso coffee
1 cinnamon stick
500 g (1 lb 2 oz) small strawberries (or halve if only large available), washed and hulled

Ricotta cream
250 g (9 oz/1 cup) ricotta cheese
75 g (2¾ oz/⅓ cup) mascarpone cheese
2 egg whites
80 g (2¾ oz/⅓ cup) caster (superfine) sugar

Place the vin santo, brown sugar, coffee and cinnamon in a small saucepan over medium–high heat and bring to the boil. Remove from the heat, add the strawberries, and set aside for 10–15 minutes, or until cooled to room temperature. Discard the cinnamon.

Meanwhile, to make the ricotta cream, push the ricotta through a fine sieve into a bowl. Add the mascarpone and whisk until well combined. Beat the egg whites in a separate bowl using electric beaters until soft peaks form. Gradually add the sugar, a spoonful at a time, and beat until thick and glossy. Fold one-third of the meringue mixture into the ricotta mixture using a metal spoon, then gently fold in the remaining meringue mixture until just combined. Cover with plastic wrap and refrigerate until required.

Divide the strawberries and vin santo syrup among six serving glasses or bowls and serve with a dollop of the ricotta cream.

Rich mocha tarts

Place the butter, flour, sugar and cocoa in the bowl of a food processor and process until the mixture resembles fine breadcrumbs. Add the egg yolk and pulse, adding 1–2 tablespoons chilled water, if necessary, until the dough just comes together. Shape the dough into a disc and cover with plastic wrap. Refrigerate for 1 hour, or until firm.

Place eight 7.5 cm (3 inch) loose-based flan (tart) tins (we used star-shaped tins) on a baking tray.

Divide the pastry into eight portions. Knead each portion on a lightly floured work surface into a smooth disc. Roll each disc into a 2 mm (1/16 inch) thick round. Line each tart tin with a pastry round, carefully pressing into the edges and base of the tin. Trim away excess pastry. Freeze for 30 minutes.

Preheat the oven to 180°C (350°F/Gas 4). Bake the tart shells for 10 minutes, or until cooked. If the bases have puffed up, gently tap down with the fingers. Cool for 10 minutes, then remove from the tins and cool completely.

To make the mocha filling, combine the cream and coffee in a small saucepan and bring to scalding point. Place the chocolate in a heatproof bowl. Strain the hot cream through a fine sieve onto the chocolate and stir until the chocolate has melted. Cool to room temperature.

Spoon the filling into each tart shell and chill for 30 minutes or until set. Remove from the refrigerator 10 minutes before serving.

MAKES 8

100 g (3½ oz) unsalted butter, chilled and cut into cubes
125 g (4½ oz/1 cup) plain (all-purpose) flour
55 g (2 oz/¼ cup) caster (superfine) sugar
30 g (1 oz/¼ cup) unsweetened cocoa powder
1 egg yolk

Mocha filling
350 ml (12 fl oz) cream
1 tablespoon coarsely ground espresso coffee beans
250 g (9 oz) dark chocolate, chopped

107

Espresso martini

SERVES 2

6 chocolate-coated coffee beans
205 g (7¼ oz/1½ cups) ice, crushed
90 ml (3 fl oz) vanilla-infused vodka
1½ tablespoons Tia Maria
½ teaspoon coffee extract

Place the coffee beans in the base of two chilled martini glasses. Combine the ice, vodka, Tia Maria and coffee extract in a cocktail shaker, shake vigorously and strain into the prepared glasses. Serve.

Tiramisù cups

Whip the cream in a large bowl using electric beaters until soft peaks form. Beat the egg yolks and sugar in a separate bowl until pale and thick. Add the mascarpone and beat until incorporated. Add the whipped cream and continue beating until stiff peaks form. Whisk the egg whites in a third bowl until soft peaks form. Fold the egg whites into the cream mixture until just combined.

Place eight 250ml (9 fl oz/1 cup) capacity cups or bowls on a tray. Combine the coffee and Kahlua in a shallow bowl. Dip the halved biscuits, one at a time, in the coffee mixture, turning once, to soak up the liquid without becoming soggy. Arrange two biscuit halves snugly in the base of each cup or bowl, then top with a heaped tablespoon of the cream mixture. Continue layering two more times, finishing with a layer of the cream mixture. Cover with plastic wrap and refrigerate overnight.

To serve, dust the tops with the cocoa.

MAKES 8

300 ml (10½ fl oz) whipping cream
3 eggs, separated
115 g (4 oz/½ cup) caster (superfine) sugar
250 g (9 oz) mascarpone cheese
250 ml (9 fl oz/1 cup) freshly made strong
    espresso coffee
80 ml (2½ fl oz/⅓ cup) Kahlua
24 small savoiardi (lady fingers), broken in half
sweetened cocoa powder, sifted, for dusting

Sticky marmalade and coffee puddings with coffee anglaise

MAKES 6

160 g (5¾ oz/½ cup) orange marmalade
150 g (5½ oz) unsalted butter, softened
155 g (5½ oz/⅔ cup) soft brown sugar
2 eggs
finely grated zest of 1 orange
2 tablespoons freshly made strong espresso coffee, cooled
125 g (4½ oz/1 cup) self-raising flour, sifted
½ teaspoon ground ginger, sifted

Coffee anglaise
5 egg yolks
115 g (4 oz/½ cup) caster (superfine) sugar
500 ml (17 fl oz/2 cups) milk
2 tablespoons espresso coffee beans, lightly crushed
½ vanilla bean, split lengthways and seeds scraped

To make the coffee anglaise, place the egg yolks and sugar in a large bowl and beat using electric beaters until pale and thick. Combine the milk, coffee, vanilla bean and seeds in a saucepan over medium heat and bring to scalding point. Gradually whisk the hot milk into the egg mixture. Return to the clean saucepan and stir with a wooden spoon over medium heat until the custard thickens and coats the back of the spoon. Remove from the heat and strain through a fine sieve into a bowl. Cool, cover the surface of the custard with plastic wrap and refrigerate until required.

Preheat the oven to 180°C (350°F/Gas 4). Grease six 200 ml (7 fl oz) capacity pudding basins (moulds). Divide the marmalade among the basins.

Cream the butter and sugar in a large bowl using electric beaters until pale and fluffy. Beat in the eggs, one at a time, beating well after each addition. Stir in the orange zest and coffee, then fold in the flour and ground ginger. Divide the batter evenly among the prepared basins—the batter will half fill the basins—and smooth the surface with the back of a spoon. Cut out six pieces of baking paper, fold a thin pleat down the middle of each one, place over each basin and tie with kitchen string.

Place the puddings in a baking tin, pour in enough boiling water to come halfway up the side of the basins. Bake for 25–30 minutes, or until a skewer inserted into the centre of a pudding comes out clean. Remove from the water bath and stand for 5 minutes before removing the paper. Invert the puddings onto serving plates and serve with the coffee anglaise.

Nougat and coffee semifreddo cones

MAKES 12

3 eggs
2 egg yolks
115 g (4 oz/½ cup) caster (superfine) sugar
1 teaspoon natural vanilla extract
600 ml (21 fl oz) whipping cream
2 tablespoons freshly made strong espresso coffee, cooled
1 tablespoon amaretto
150 g (5½ oz) almond nougat, finely chopped

Cherries in syrup
160 g (5¾ oz/½ cup) cherry jam
2 tablespoons Grand Marnier
36 cherries, stems intact

Almond praline
110 g (3¾ oz/1 cup) whole almonds, toasted and roughly chopped
165 g (5¾ oz/¾ cup) sugar

Cut out twelve 30 cm (12 inch) squares of baking paper. Fold each square in half to form a triangle and, using the centre of the longest edge of the triangle as the cone axis point, twist the paper to form a cone shape, then secure with a staple.

Place the eggs, egg yolks, sugar and vanilla in a large heatproof bowl over a saucepan of simmering water and beat using electric beaters for 4–5 minutes or until pale and frothy. Remove from the heat and continue to beat until the mixture cools and is pale and thick. Whip the cream in a separate bowl using electric beaters until soft peaks form. Fold in the coffee and amaretto. Fold the cream into the custard mixture, then fold in the nougat. Spoon the mixture into the prepared paper cones and stand upright in tall glasses. Place in the freezer for 4 hours, or until firm.

To make the cherries in syrup, combine the jam, Grand Marnier and 60 ml (2 fl oz/¼ cup) water in a saucepan and stir over low heat until the jam has melted. Remove from the heat, add the cherries and swirl. Set aside to cool.

To make the almond praline, spread the almonds on a baking tray lined with baking paper. Place the sugar and 60 ml (2 fl oz/¼ cup) water in a heavy-based saucepan over medium heat and stir to dissolve the sugar. Bring to the boil and simmer, without stirring, until the caramel turns a deep amber colour. Pour over the nuts and spread evenly. Allow to cool and harden. Break into shards or crush until the consistency of coarse breadcrumbs using a mortar and pestle or food processor.

Carefully remove the paper from each semifreddo cone and invert the semifreddo onto a serving plate. Spoon the cherries around the semifreddo and drizzle on the syrup. Alternatively, decorate with shards of praline or sprinkle with crushed praline, as desired.

Panettone, rum and coffee puddings

Preheat the oven to 180°C (350°F/Gas 4). Lightly grease eight 125 ml (4 fl oz/½ cup) capacity ovenproof dishes.

Divide the panettone between the prepared dishes. Whisk the eggs, caster sugar and liquor in a large bowl to combine.

Place the milk, cream and coffee in a saucepan over medium–high heat and bring to scalding point. Remove from the heat. Gradually whisk the hot milk mixture into the egg mixture until well combined. Strain the mixture through a fine sieve into a jug, then pour over the panettone. Set aside for 10 minutes to allow the panettone to absorb the custard.

Place the dishes in a baking tin and pour in enough boiling water to come halfway up the side of the dishes. Bake for 30–40 minutes, or until puffed and golden brown and a knife inserted into the centre of a pudding comes out clean.

Dust the puddings with the icing sugar and serve warm with the ice cream.

MAKES 8

300 g (10½ oz) panettone, torn into rough 3 cm (1¼ inch) pieces
3 eggs
55 g (2 oz/¼ cup) caster (superfine) sugar
2½ tablespoons dark rum, bourbon or whisky
300 ml (10½ fl oz) milk
250 g (9 oz) thick (double/heavy) cream
2 tablespoons finely ground espresso coffee beans
icing (confectioners') sugar, sifted, for dusting
good quality vanilla ice cream, to serve

119

Café brûlot

SERVES 6

1 cinnamon stick
zest of ½ lemon, white pith removed
zest of ½ orange, white pith removed
1 teaspoon whole cloves
2 tablespoons caster (superfine) sugar, plus
extra to sweeten
60 ml (2 fl oz/¼ cup) Grand Marnier
125 ml (4 fl oz/½ cup) Cognac
750 ml (26 fl oz/3 cups) freshly made strong,
hot espresso coffee
whipped cream, to serve
thinly sliced orange zest, to serve

Combine the cinnamon, lemon and orange zest, cloves, sugar, Grand Marnier and 80 ml (2½ fl oz/⅓ cup) of the Cognac in a saucepan over medium heat and stir until the sugar has dissolved and the mixture is just simmering. Remove from the heat. Pour in the remaining Cognac and carefully light the mixture. Allow the flames to die down, pour in the coffee and mix to combine. Strain and pour into six coffee cups or heatproof glasses. Serve immediately with a dollop of whipped cream and strips of orange zest. Sweeten to taste with extra sugar, if desired.

Espresso soufflé

To make the crème pâtissière, place the milk and coffee beans in a saucepan over medium heat and bring to scalding point. Remove from the heat and set aside to infuse for 10 minutes. Beat the egg yolks and sugar in a bowl using electric beaters until pale and thick. Add the flour and mix well. Strain the milk through a fine sieve and whisk into the egg mixture. Return the mixture to the clean saucepan over medium heat and whisk constantly until the mixture thickens and just comes to the boil. Transfer the mixture to a bowl, add the vanilla and whisk for 1 minute to cool a little. Cover with plastic wrap and refrigerate until chilled.

Preheat the oven to 200°C (400°F/Gas 6). Butter six 150 ml (5 fl oz) capacity soufflé moulds and lightly dust with 2 tablespoons of the caster sugar.

Whisk the egg whites in a large bowl using electric beaters until soft peaks form. Gradually add the remaining caster sugar and whisk until the sugar has dissolved and stiff peaks form. Use a metal spoon to fold one-third of the egg whites into the crème pâtissière, then gently fold in the remaining egg whites until just combined. Carefully spoon the soufflé mixture into the prepared moulds, fill to the rim and flatten the tops with a knife. Bake for 12–15 minutes, or until risen. Serve immediately, dusted with the icing sugar.

MAKES 6

3 tablespoons caster (superfine) sugar
6 egg whites
icing (confectioners') sugar, sifted, for dusting

Crème pâtissière
250 ml (9 fl oz/1 cup) milk
40 g (1½ oz/½ cup) espresso coffee beans
3 egg yolks
80 g (2¾ oz/⅓ cup) caster (superfine) sugar
35 g (1¼ oz) plain (all-purpose) flour
½ teaspoon natural vanilla extract

123

Coconut ice with coffee syrup

MAKES 6

100 g (3½ oz) palm sugar (jaggery), chopped
2 kaffir lime (makrut) leaves, finely sliced
400 ml (14 fl oz) coconut milk
20 g (¾ oz/⅓ cup) flaked coconut, lightly toasted

Coffee syrup
230 g (8¼ oz/1 cup) caster (superfine) sugar
60 ml (2 fl oz/¼ cup) freshly made
espresso coffee
1 tablespoon white rum (optional)

Place the palm sugar, kaffir lime leaves and 125 ml (4 fl oz/½ cup) water in a small saucepan over medium–high heat, stirring to dissolve the sugar, boil for 1 minute. Remove from the heat and set aside to cool. Place the coconut milk in a bowl. Strain the cooled syrup into the milk, discarding the leaves, and stir to mix well. Pour into six 125 ml (4 fl oz/½ cup) capacity dariole moulds. Cover and freeze for 4 hours, or until frozen.

To make the coffee syrup, combine the sugar and 2½ tablespoons water in a small heavy-based saucepan over high heat and stir to dissolve the sugar. Simmer, without stirring, for 5–8 minutes, or until the syrup is a pale caramel colour. Remove from the heat and stir in the coffee and rum, if using. Set aside to cool.

To serve, dip each mould in hot water and invert onto a serving plate. Drizzle the coffee syrup over the top and sprinkle on the coconut flakes.

Self-saucing coffee and chocolate puddings

Preheat the oven to 180°C (350°F/Gas 4). Grease six 200 ml (7 fl oz) capacity ovenproof dishes and place on a baking tray.

Sift the flour, cocoa and sugar into a bowl. Place the butter, milk and egg in a jug and whisk to combine. Pour the egg mixture onto the dry ingredients and stir until well combined. Stir in the chocolate and spoon the mixture into the prepared dishes.

To make the sauce, combine the sugar and cocoa in a bowl and sprinkle evenly over each pudding. Stir the Tia Maria into the coffee and carefully pour about 2 tablespoons over each pudding. Bake for 20 minutes, or until the puddings are puffed in the centre and firm to touch. Serve immediately with the ice cream or cream.

NOTE: To serve eight, use 150 ml (5 fl oz) capacity ovenproof dishes.

MAKES 6

125 g (4½ oz/1 cup) self-raising flour
2 tablespoons unsweetened cocoa powder
115 g (4 oz/½ cup) caster (superfine) sugar
60 g (2¼ oz/¼ cup) unsalted butter, melted
125 ml (4½ fl oz/½ cup) milk
1 egg, lightly beaten
50 g (1¾ oz) dark chocolate, chopped
good quality vanilla ice cream or thick
 (double/heavy) cream, to serve

Sauce
140 g (5 oz/¾ cup) soft brown sugar
2 tablespoons unsweetened cocoa powder, sifted
1 tablespoon Tia Maria
250 ml (9 fl oz/1 cup) freshly made, hot
 espresso coffee

Espresso granita with sambuca

SERVES 6

220 g (7¾ oz/1 cup) sugar
1 tablespoon aniseeds
3 x 5 cm (1¼ inch) strips lemon zest, white pith removed
500 ml (17 fl oz/2 cups) freshly made strong espresso coffee
black sambuca, to serve

Place the sugar, aniseeds, lemon zest and 500 ml (17 fl oz/2 cups) water in a saucepan over medium–high heat, stirring to dissolve the sugar. Bring to the boil and stir in the coffee. Remove from the heat and set aside to cool to room temperature.

Strain the coffee mixture through a fine sieve into a 20 x 30 cm (8 x 12 inch) baking tin, cover and place in the freezer. After 1 hour, stir the mixture, using a fork to drag the ice crystals from the edges of the container into the centre. Return to the freezer and repeat this process every 30 minutes to break up the mixture and form crystal flakes. The entire process takes 3–4 hours.

Serve the espresso granita in six chilled glasses accompanied by shots of sambuca.

Macaroons with coffee cream and poached apricots

MAKES 12

8 egg whites
345 g (12 oz/1½ cups) caster (superfine) sugar
2 teaspoons white wine vinegar
1 teaspoon natural vanilla extract
1 tablespoon ground hazelnuts
2 tablespoons icing (confectioners') sugar, sifted,
for dusting
150 g (5½ oz) hazelnuts, toasted and skinned

Coffee cream
½ gelatine sheet
3 egg yolks
2 tablespoons caster (superfine) sugar
2 tablespoons freshly made espresso
coffee, cooled
115 g (4 oz/½ cup) thick (double/heavy) cream

Poached apricots
125 ml (4 fl oz/½ cup) freshly squeezed
orange juice
125 ml (4 fl oz/½ cup) Marsala
1 vanilla bean, split lengthways
115 g (4 oz/½ cup) caster (superfine) sugar
12 firm, ripe apricots

Preheat the oven to 160°C (315°F/Gas 2–3). Line the base and sides of a 20 x 30 cm (8 x 12 inch) baking tin with baking paper.

To make the coffee cream, soak the gelatine sheet in a bowl of cold water until softened. Place the egg yolks and sugar in a large heatproof bowl and beat using electric beaters until pale and thick, then stir in the coffee. Meanwhile, place the cream in a small saucepan over medium heat and bring to scalding point. Gradually whisk the hot cream into the egg yolk mixture. Sit the bowl over a saucepan of gently simmering water, ensuring the bowl does not touch the water, and cook, stirring, until the mixture thickens and coats the back of a spoon. Remove the bowl from the heat. Squeeze the softened gelatine leaf to remove any excess water, add to the hot cream mixture and stir to dissolve. Set aside to cool. Cover with plastic wrap and refrigerate until firm.

To make the poached apricots, place the orange juice, Marsala, vanilla, sugar, apricots and 125 ml (4 fl oz/ ½ cup) water in a saucepan over medium–high heat and stir to dissolve the sugar. Simmer, stirring occasionally, for 15 minutes, or until the apricots are tender. Remove the apricots and set aside. Bring the poaching liquid to a simmer and cook until syrupy and reduced by half. Strain through a fine sieve into a jug, discarding the solids, and set aside to cool. Halve the apricots, remove stones and return the fruit to the syrup.

Meanwhile, whisk the egg whites in a large bowl using electric beaters until soft peaks form. Gradually add the sugar, a spoonful at a time, and whisk until thick and glossy. Gently fold in the vinegar, vanilla and ground hazelnuts. Spread the macaroon mixture into the prepared tin. Bake for 25 minutes. Cool for 2 minutes in the tin, then invert onto a sheet of baking paper dusted with the icing sugar. Allow to cool completely. Peel off the baking paper.

Place the hazelnuts in the bowl of a food processor and process to coarse crumbs. Spread the crushed hazelnuts on a plate. Carefully cut out 12 rounds from the macaroon using a 6 cm (2½ inch) cookie cutter.

Roll each macaroon round over the hazelnuts to coat the edges evenly.

Place the macaroons, icing sugar dusted side up, on serving plates and spoon the apricots and poaching syrup over the top. Serve with a small bowl or a dollop of coffee cream alongside.

Coffee choc-tops

MAKES 12

6 egg yolks
200 g (7 oz) caster (superfine) sugar
125 ml (4 fl oz/½ cup) freshly made strong
espresso coffee
500 ml (17 fl oz/2 cups) cream
250 ml (9 fl oz/1 cup) milk
12 mini waffle cones
150 g (5½ oz) dark chocolate, chopped
35 g (1¼ oz) Copha (white vegetable shortening)
50 g (1¾ oz) peanut and chocolate slab bar,
finely crushed

Beat the egg yolks and sugar in a large heatproof bowl using electric beaters until pale and thick. Combine the coffee and cream in a saucepan over medium heat and bring to scalding point. Gradually pour the hot cream over the egg yolk mixture, whisking continuously until well combined. Sit the bowl over a saucepan of gently simmering water and continue to whisk until the mixture thickens and coats the back of a wooden spoon. Remove from the heat and strain the custard through a fine sieve into a bowl or jug. Cover with plastic wrap and set aside to cool.

Stir the milk into the custard. Churn the custard mixture in an ice-cream machine according to the manufacturer's instructions. Transfer to an airtight container and freeze for 2 hours, or until firm. Scoop the ice cream into the cones and stand upright in cups in the freezer for at least 1 hour.

Melt the chocolate and Copha in a small saucepan over low heat and transfer to a small bowl. Working with one cone at a time, hold the base of the cone, dip the ice cream end into the melted chocolate mixture, then quickly sprinkle on the crushed chocolate bar. Repeat with the remaining cones. Serve immediately or return to the freezer until ready to serve.

Espresso zabaglione with fennel seed wafers

Preheat the oven to 160°C (315°F/Gas 2–3). Grease two baking trays.

To make the fennel seed wafers, combine the butter, honey and sugar in a small saucepan over low heat and stir until the butter has melted. Remove from the heat. Sift together the flour and ground fennel and stir into the butter mixture with a wooden spoon. Stir in the egg white to combine. Place teaspoons of the mixture onto the prepared trays, 5 cm (2 inches) apart to allow for spreading, and scatter the fennel seeds over the top. Bake for 6–8 minutes, or until golden. Cool for 1 minute on the trays, then use a spatula to transfer the wafers to a wire rack to cool completely and become crisp.

Whisk the egg yolks and sugar in a large heatproof bowl over a saucepan of simmering water until pale, thick and doubled in volume. Gradually whisk in the combined coffee and Marsala and continue to whisk for 8–10 minutes, or until creamy and thick. Remove from the heat and whisk until the zabaglione cools down slightly. Serve warm with the fennel seed wafers.

The wafers will keep, stored in an airtight container, for up to 2 days.

SERVES 6

6 egg yolks
115 g (4 oz/½ cup) caster (superfine) sugar
125 ml (4 fl oz/½ cup) freshly made strong espresso coffee
60 ml (2 fl oz/¼ cup) Marsala

Fennel seed wafers
50 g (1¾ oz) unsalted butter
1½ tablespoons honey
2 tablespoons soft brown sugar
2 tablespoons plain (all-purpose) flour
½ teaspoon ground fennel
1 egg white, lightly beaten
1 tablespoon fennel seeds, lightly crushed

Amaretti and coffee custard puddings

MAKES 6

250 ml (9 fl oz/1 cup) milk
125 ml (4 fl oz/½ cup) cream
2 tablespoons freshly made strong espresso coffee
4 eggs
115 g (4 oz/½ cup) caster (superfine) sugar
75 g (2¾ oz) amaretti biscuits (cookies), crumbled

Preheat the oven to 180°C (350°F/Gas 4).

Place the milk, cream and coffee in a saucepan over medium heat and bring to scalding point. Remove from the heat and set aside to infuse for 5 minutes.

Beat the eggs and sugar in a large bowl using electric beaters until pale and thick. Add the milk mixture and whisk until well combined. Scoop off any excess foam, then divide the mixture among six 150 ml (3¾ fl oz) capacity ramekins and transfer the dishes to a baking tin. Add enough boiling water to the tin to come halfway up the side of the ramekins. Bake for 25–30 minutes, or until the puddings are just set and have a slight wobble in the centre. Remove from the water bath and set aside to cool. Sprinkle the amaretti over the custards and serve warm or at room temperature.

Frangelico affogato

Place scoops of the ice cream in six small glass bowls and sprinkle on the hazelnuts. Pour the Frangelico into six shot glasses. Arrange each bowl of ice cream, shot glass of Frangelico and shot of espresso on a serving plate. To serve, pour the Frangelico and coffee over the ice cream.

Serve with almond espresso biscotti (page 9), if desired.

SERVES 6

1 litre (35 fl oz/4 cups) good quality vanilla ice cream
70 g (2½ oz/½ cup) hazelnuts, toasted, skinned and roughly chopped
185 ml (6 fl oz/¾ cup) Frangelico
6 single espresso coffee shots

Short black mousse cups

MAKES 6

120 g (4¼ oz) dark chocolate, chopped
20 g (¾ oz) unsalted butter
4 eggs, separated
2 teaspoons instant coffee granules dissolved in
1 tablespoon hot water
1 tablespoon dark rum (optional)
1 tablespoon caster (superfine) sugar
sweetened cocoa powder, sifted, for dusting

Melt the chocolate in a heatproof bowl over a saucepan of simmering water, ensuring the bowl does not touch the water. Remove the bowl from the heat, add the butter and whisk until the mixture is melted and smooth. Stir in the egg yolks, one at a time. Stir in the coffee and rum, if using. Set aside to cool.

Whisk the egg whites in a large bowl using electric beaters until soft peaks form. Add the sugar and continue to whisk until stiff peaks form. Gently fold the egg whites into the chocolate mixture until just combined. Spoon the mixture into six espresso cups or glasses and refrigerate for at least 2 hours, or until firm. To serve, dust the tops lightly with the cocoa.

Dried fruit compote with coffee liqueur

Combine the sugar, Tia Maria, coffee, vanilla and cinnamon in a saucepan over medium heat and stir to dissolve the sugar. Simmer for 10 minutes, or until the mixture becomes syrupy. Add the dried fruit and cook for a further 10 minutes, or until the fruit is soft and the syrup is reduced by half. Remove from the heat and set aside to cool to room temperature. Serve in bowls topped with a dollop of the cream.

The compote will keep, stored in an airtight container in the refrigerator, for up to 1 week.

SERVES 6

145 g (5¼ oz/⅔ cup) caster (superfine) sugar
250 ml (9 fl oz/1 cup) Tia Maria
80 ml (2½ fl oz/⅓ cup) freshly made
   espresso coffee
½ vanilla bean
1 cinnamon stick
100 g (3½ oz) pitted prunes
6 dried figs
12 dried apricot halves
thick (double/heavy) cream, to serve

Vanilla panna cotta with coffee jelly

MAKES 6

2 gelatine sheets
750 ml (26 fl oz/3 cups) cream
115 g (4 oz/½ cup) caster (superfine) sugar
1 vanilla bean, split lengthways
6 coffee beans
5 cm (2 inch) strip lemon zest, white pith removed

Coffee jelly
1 gelatine sheet
125 ml (4 fl oz/½ cup) freshly made hot espresso coffee
1 tablespoon caster (superfine) sugar
1 tablespoon bourbon

Soak the gelatine sheets in a bowl of cold water for 5 minutes, or until softened. Combine the cream, sugar, vanilla bean, coffee beans and lemon zest in a saucepan over medium heat and bring to scalding point, stirring to dissolve the sugar. Remove from the heat. Squeeze the softened gelatine sheets to remove any excess water, add to the hot cream mixture and stir until the gelatine has dissolved. Strain through a fine sieve into a jug and scrape in the vanilla seeds. Discard the vanilla bean.

Pour the vanilla cream mixture into six 200 ml (7 fl oz) glasses. Refrigerate for 4 hours, or overnight, to set.

To make the coffee jelly, soak the gelatine sheet in a bowl of cold water for 5 minutes, or until softened. Squeeze the excess water from the softened gelatine sheet. Combine the gelatine and hot coffee in a bowl and stir until the gelatine has dissolved. Add the sugar and bourbon and stir until the sugar has dissolved. Set aside to cool to room temperature.

Carefully pour a 5 mm (¼ inch) layer of the coffee jelly over the set panna cotta. Return to the refrigerator for 2 hours, or until the jelly has set.

Turkish coffee and date brûlée

MAKES 6

60 ml (2 fl oz/¼ cup) freshly squeezed
orange juice
55 g (2 oz/¼ cup) soft brown sugar
75 g (2¾ oz) fresh dates, seeds removed and
chopped into 1 cm (½ inch) pieces
1 tablespoon finely ground Turkish coffee beans
6 cardamom pods, lightly crushed
30 cm (12 inch) square piece muslin
500 ml (17 fl oz/2 cups) cream
4 egg yolks
¼ teaspoon ground cardamom
4 tablespoons caster (superfine) sugar

Combine the orange juice and brown sugar in a saucepan over low heat and stir to dissolve the sugar. Add the dates and cook for 3–5 minutes, or until the dates are soft and the syrup is absorbed, adding a little water if the mixture becomes too dry. Set aside to cool.

Place the coffee and cardamom pods in the double folded muslin and tie with kitchen string to secure. Place the muslin bag and cream in a small saucepan over medium–high heat and bring to scalding point. Remove from the heat and set aside to infuse for 5 minutes. Squeeze the muslin bag to extract as much of the coffee-flavoured cream as possible, then discard.

Using electric beaters beat the egg yolks, ground cardamom and half the caster sugar in a large heatproof bowl until pale and thick. Whisk the hot cream into the egg yolk mixture. Place the bowl over a saucepan of gently simmering water, ensuring the bowl does not touch the water, and stir with a wooden spoon until the mixture thickens and coats the back of the spoon. Transfer the bowl to a sink of cold water and whisk until the custard cools to room temperature.

Preheat the grill (broiler) to high. Divide the date mixture among six 100 ml (3½ fl oz) capacity heatproof glasses and spoon in the coffee and cardamom custard. Refrigerate for 2 hours to set. Sprinkle on the remaining caster sugar and place under the grill until the sugar has caramelised. Serve immediately.

Index

Published in 2010 by Murdoch Books Pty Limited

Murdoch Books Australia
Pier 8/9
23 Hickson Road
Millers Point NSW 2000
Phone: +61 (0) 2 8220 2000
Fax: +61 (0) 2 8220 2558
www.murdochbooks.com.au

Murdoch Books UK Limited
Erico House, 6th Floor
93–99 Upper Richmond Road
Putney, London SW15 2TG
Phone: +44 (0) 20 8785 5995
Fax: +44 (0) 20 8785 5985
www.murdochbooks.co.uk

Publisher: Jane Lawson
Photographer: Brett Stevens
Stylist: Matt Page
Project manager: Livia Caiazzo
Editor: Megan Johnston
Food editor: Chrissy Freer
Design concept: Reuben Crossman
Design layout: Helen Beard
Recipes by: the Murdoch Books test kitchen
Production: Kita George

Text, design and photography copyright © 2009
Murdoch Books

National Library of Australia Cataloguing-in-Publication Data
Title: Indulgence Coffee: a fine selection of sweet treats
ISBN: 9781741965148 (hbk)
Series: Indulgence series
Notes: Includes index
Subjects: cake
Dewey Number: 641.865

A catalogue record for this book is available from the
British Library.

Colour separation by SPLITTING IMAGE.

PRINTED IN CHINA.

IMPORTANT: Those who might be at risk from the effects of
salmonella poisoning (the elderly, pregnant women, young
children and those suffering from immune deficiency
diseases) should consult their doctor with any concerns about
eating raw eggs.

OVEN GUIDE: You may find cooking times vary depending
on the oven you are using. For fan-forced ovens, as a general
rule, set the oven temperature to 20°C (35°F) lower than
indicated in the recipe.